Blastoff! Readers are carefully developed by literacy experts to build reading stamina and move students toward fluency by combining standards-based content with developmentally appropriate text.

Level 1 provides the most support through repetition of high-frequency words, light text, predictable sentence patterns, and strong visual support.

Level 2 offers early readers a bit more challenge through varied sentences, increased text load, and text-supportive special features.

Level 3 advances early-fluent readers toward fluency through increased text load, less reliance on photos, advancing concepts, longer sentences, and more complex special features.

★ **Blastoff! Universe**

This edition first published in 2026 by Bellwether Media, Inc.

No part of this publication may be reproduced in whole or in part without written permission of the publisher. For information regarding permission, write to Bellwether Media, Inc., Attention: Permissions Department, 3500 American Blvd W, Suite 150, Bloomington, MN 55431.

Library of Congress Cataloging-in-Publication Data

LC record for Hungary available at: https://lccn.loc.gov/2025014991

Text copyright © 2026 by Bellwether Media, Inc. BLASTOFF! READERS and associated logos are trademarks and/or registered trademarks of Bellwether Media, Inc. Bellwether Media is a division of FlutterBee Education Group.

Editor: Betsy Rathburn   Designer: Laura Sowers

Printed in the United States of America, North Mankato, MN.

Table of Contents

All About Hungary	4
Land and Animals	6
Life in Hungary	12
Hungary Facts	20
Glossary	22
To Learn More	23
Index	24

All About Hungary

Budapest

Hungary is a **landlocked** country in central Europe. Its capital city is Budapest.

Hungary is known for its **folk music** and **hot springs**.

Land and Animals

Most of Hungary is flat. The Great Hungarian **Plain** covers the east. Hills and mountains lie in the west.

The Danube River flows through the center of the country.

Great Hungarian Plain

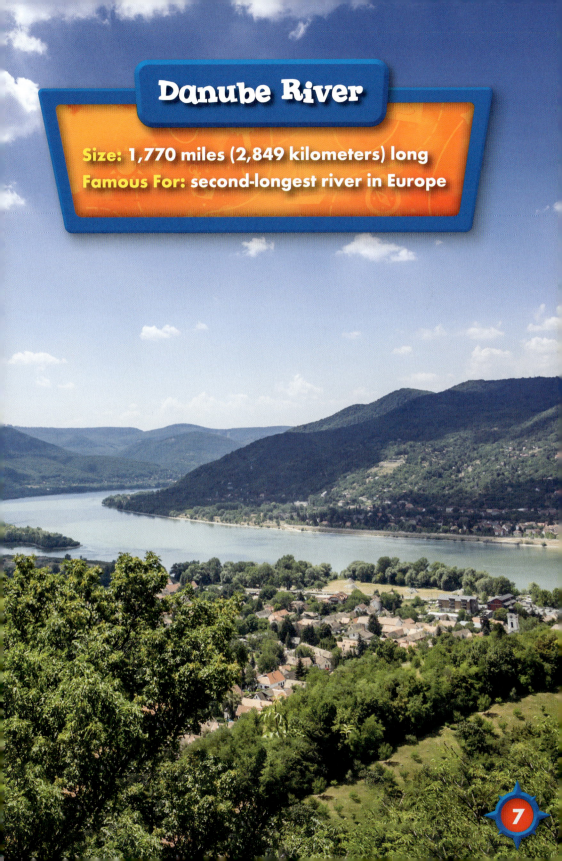

Danube River

Size: 1,770 miles (2,849 kilometers) long
Famous For: second-longest river in Europe

Hungary is a dry country.
Summer is the rainiest season.
It is hot.

Winter is cold and sometimes snowy. Spring and fall are mild.

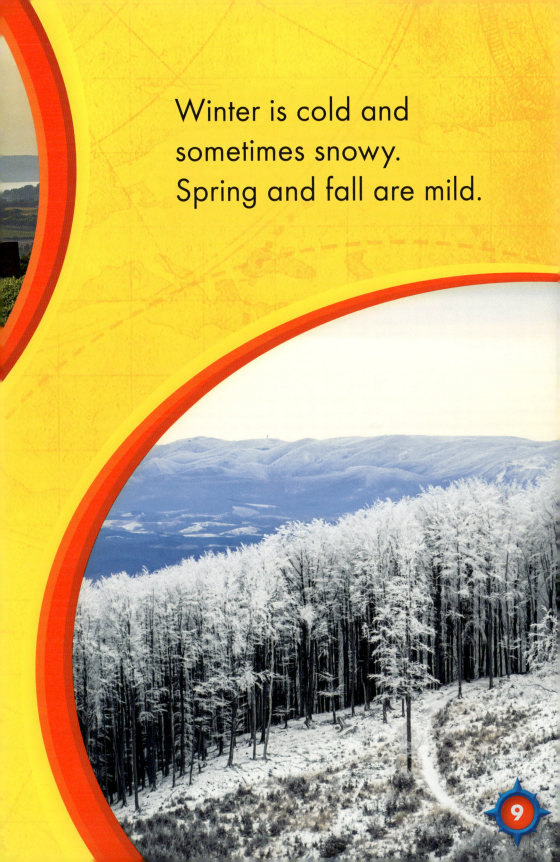

Roe deer **graze** on the plain.
Wolves and jackals hunt in forests.

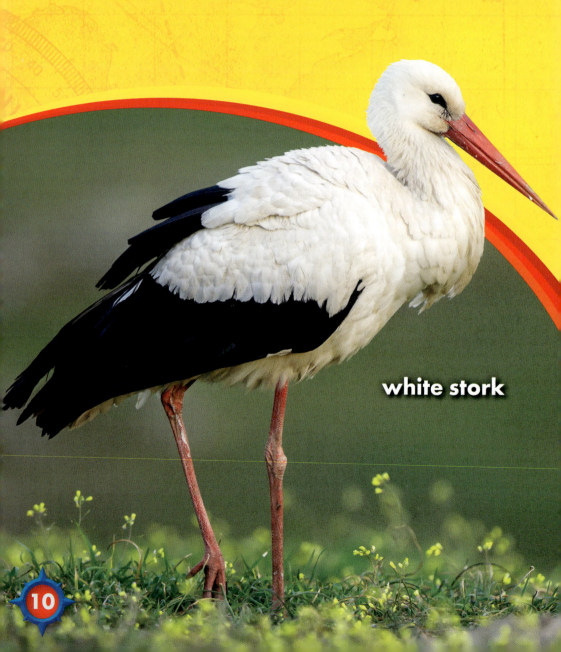

white stork

Animals of Hungary

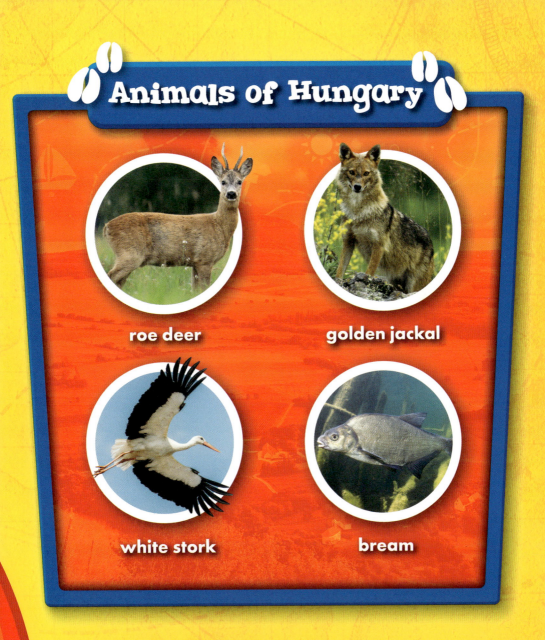

roe deer

golden jackal

white stork

bream

White storks nest near **wetlands**. Bream and pike swim in lakes and rivers.

Life in Hungary

Most people have a Hungarian **background**. They speak Hungarian. **Immigrants** also live and work in Hungary.

Many people are **Catholic**.

Many Hungarians enjoy sports. Soccer is common. Baths warmed by hot springs are popular places to visit.

People also play and dance to folk music.

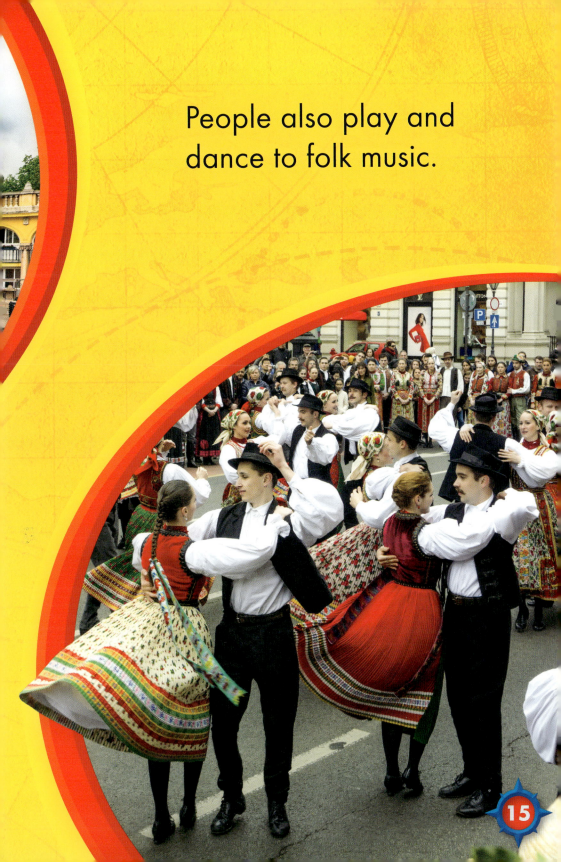

Sour cherry soup is often eaten before summertime meals. Goulash is a favorite meat stew.

Hungarian Foods

sour cherry soup

goulash

chicken paprikash

Dobos torta

goulash

Chicken paprikash is made with **paprika**. *Dobos torta* is a rich chocolate cake.

Each year, people gather for music and art at the Budapest Spring **Festival**.

Easter is a big holiday. People share beautiful painted eggs. Hungarians love to **celebrate**!

Easter

Hungary Facts

Size:
35,918 square miles
(93,028 square kilometers)

Population:
9,855,745 (2024)

National Holiday:
Saint Stephen's Day (August 20)

Main Language:
Hungarian

Capital City:
Budapest

Famous Face

Name: Ernő Rubik

Famous For: invented the Rubik's Cube in 1974

Religions

- Protestant: 12%
- none: 16%
- Catholic: 30%
- other: 42%

Top Landmarks

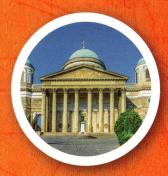

Esztergom Basilica

Hungarian Parliament

Széchenyi Baths

Glossary

background—people's experiences, knowledge, and family history

Catholic—relating to the Christian church that is led by the pope

celebrate—to do something special or fun for an event, occasion, or holiday

festival—a time or event of celebration

folk music—the traditional music of the people in a country or region

graze—to eat grasses and other plants on the ground

hot springs—places where warm water flows out of the ground

immigrants—people who move to a new country

landlocked—enclosed or nearly enclosed by land

paprika—powder from a pepper that is used as a spice in cooking

plain—an area of flat land with few trees

wetlands—areas of land that are covered with low levels of water for most of the year

To Learn More

AT THE LIBRARY

Barnes, Rachael. *Germany*. Minneapolis, Minn.: Bellwether Media, 2023.

Pettiford, Rebecca. *Austria*. Minneapolis, Minn.: Bellwether Media, 2026.

Spanier, Kristine. *Hungary*. Minneapolis, Minn.: Jump!, 2022.

ON THE WEB

FACTSURFER

Factsurfer.com gives you a safe, fun way to find more information.

1. Go to www.factsurfer.com.
2. Enter "Hungary" into the search box and click 🔍.
3. Select your book cover to see a list of related content.

Index

animals, 10, 11
baths, 14
Budapest, 4, 5
Budapest Spring Festival, 18, 19
capital (see Budapest)
Catholic, 12
Danube River, 6, 7
Easter, 18
Europe, 4
fall, 9
folk music, 5, 15
food, 16, 17
forests, 10
Great Hungarian Plain, 6, 10
hills, 6
hot springs, 5, 14
Hungarian, 12, 13
Hungary facts, 20–21

immigrants, 12
lakes, 11
landlocked, 4
map, 5
mountains, 6
people, 12, 14, 15, 18
rivers, 6, 7, 11
say hello, 13
soccer, 14
spring, 9
summer, 8, 16
wetlands, 11
winter, 9

The images in this book are reproduced through the courtesy of: V_E, front cover, pp. 14-15; Millenius, p. 3; Daniel Jara, pp. 4-5, 10-11; skovalsky, p. 6; Gts, pp. 6-7; andras_csontos, pp. 8-9; Matyas Levente Sipos, p. 9; Piotr Krzeslak, p. 11 (roe deer); WildMedia, p. 11 (golden jackal); Great Brut Here, p. 11 (white stork); Rostislav, p. 11 (bream); Mitzo, p. 12; Onjira Leibe, pp. 12-13; MaciejGillert, p. 14 (soccer); Andocs, p. 15; Svetlana Monyakova, p. 16 (sour cherry soup); Dar1930, p. 16 (goulash); Nagy Julia, p. 16 (chicken paprikash); AlenaKogotkova, p. 16 (*Dobas torta*); EdNurg, p. 17; Huvosi, p. 18; Andfoto/ Alamy Stock Photo, pp. 18-19; supparsorn, p. 20 (flag); dpa picture alliance/ Alamy Stock Photo, p. 20 (Ernő Rubik); dudlajzov, p. 21 (Esztergom Basilica); Mistervlad, p. 21 (Hungarian Parliament); MarKord, p. 21 (Széchenyi Baths); Eric Isselée, p. 22.

24